ALLOTMENT DAYS

ALLOTMENT DAYS
MATTHEW BIGGS

CONTENTS

INTRODUCTION

The old man leaned on his fork, scratched the stubble on his aged chin and adjusted his cap. My profile has changed, he mused, gone are the days when this was my domain, now you're just as likely to find a mother with young children, concerned that their food is 'chemical free', a manager in a high profile career seeking solace in the no-pressure zone or a gardener from Britain's diverse cultural background growing exotic produce for the table. Whoever they are, allotment gardeners have one common aim, to enjoy the freedom, camaraderie, exercise and fresh produce that allotment gardening brings. There is a cheerful acceptance of the simple pleasures in life that can be found in the open air, by sowing a few seeds in a peaceful oasis where time plods along at the pace of slow growing plants. They understand that they are all subject to a higher power that controls the sunshine and rain, bowing in deference as they plant their leeks, battle with pests and diseases and harvest the bounty of the earth. Gardening is a leisurely occupation, a great 'leveller' and no respecter of persons - we all garden under the same sky. That is why it's a noble art encouraging an understanding of our place in this world and our niche in the passage of time. It encourages sharing, helpfulness, friendliness, understanding, compassion and laughter; qualities so lacking in much of the modern world. There is little room for pride (apart from our prize winning marrows!), just a thankfulness for the bounty of the earth in an on-going harvest festival and an incurable optimism that despite the weather, next year will always be better.

They still dig for victory, some to break the shackles of supermarkets who dominate their food supply, or simply for the satisfaction of 'growing your own' – the perfect stress busting antidote to a modern life spent staring at a screen, stuck in a jam or commuting on trains.

Whatever the motivation, most allotmenteers speak of the liberation of being on their own plot where constraints are few and opportunities for self expression many. They work as the spirit moves them, grow their favourite vegetables, experiment without fear of failure, create outdoor art, keep animals, dig deep holes and it can be as neat or rough cut as their heart's desire. In an increasingly homogenised world, allotments are packed with personalities and the individual reigns supreme. They are tightly knit communities in an increasingly impersonal society, rich in characters and gardeners with vivid imagination and abundant creativity as this book reveals.

I remember visiting an allotment just outside Newcastle many years ago in an area of high unemployment, most of the lads who gardened there once worked in the shipyards and related industries that had long disappeared. Each morning, they left the house, not now to go to work but to the allotment, it became the focal point of their lives and continued the community bond that had been established at work. Lack of disposable income had encouraged ingenuity; the whole place was based on recycled materials, the ultimate in sustainable gardening that we should all now seek to achieve. The site and individual plots had been corralled with multicoloured recycled timbers to mark out territory and serve as a barrier to local vandals. Every Saturday a lorry from a nearby factory appeared and dumped materials ready for collection; pallets, polystyrene, perspex, 'off-cuts' and planks of timber in all shapes and sizes.

A few minutes after I arrived early one February morning a battalion of ghostly figures emerged through the mist from the alleyways between the plots to the rhythmic crunching of hobnail boots, scrabbled silently through the debris, claimed their booty then melted away. These materials metamorphosed on their allotments into raised beds, seats, cold frames and even DIY greenhouses; one gentleman was even using street lamp covers, from an undisclosed source, to protect his dahlia tubers and sprouting potatoes! Low rents, a few pence for a packet of seeds and some fertiliser make allotments achievable for all and that's the allure. No wonder there's a joyous resurgence of interest after years of neglect and times they are a-changing. Many once solitary sites are now vibrant, waiting lists are commonplace and new housing estates are being developed with 'child friendly' allotments incorporating paddling pools and sand pits. In most parts of Britain, demand is booming, the Green Party on the Greater London Assembly is demanding action to increase the number of allotments in London as a rise in mass density housing is set to increase the demand. Yet despite their popularity there are still problems, with several cases of claimed unreasonable rent rises, in one case, a staggering 300% per year and property developers still lurk menacingly in the shadows despite the increased lobbying power of Societies and Associations. Some sites have been lost though this is not always detrimental. In many cases it has helped to secure the future and improve the facilities of more popular sites, yet many still believe they all should be retained as a matter of principle.

It is only a matter of a few centuries since the Industrial revolution drew us in droves from the countryside to live in city squalor and work in factories in the name of progress, suppressing our natural urge to dig and delve. Now in the early 21st century we are breaking free from the artificiality of city life to sink our teeth into plump tomatoes, tender beans and savour succulent sweetcorn that can be rushed straight from the plot to the pot without plastic packaging or a lorry in sight! Flavour is at the forefront encouraged by a new wave of enthusiasm for the culinary arts. Allotments are the new gym, the 'in' place to exercise and the rewards are delicious too. Bend slowly and touch your toes, stretch to the left and then to the right now breathe deeply and relax, feel yourself in harmony with nature and the earth on which you stand. Now pick up your spade, rest the edge of the blade on the ground and Push! There's no doubt, that for all of the finest reasons, we're all diggin' allotments. Long may they flourish!

Matthew Biggs

TOP OF THE PLOTS

"Try to add eye catching extras, there are marigolds around my plot, a patch of wildflowers, lilies in a pot outside the polytunnel and hanging baskets on the shed" advises Veronica Collicutt, Britain's first female National Allotment Champion who only took on a plot because her garden was too small.

"I aim for the best of everything, the seed is high quality for good germination, only the best plants are saved then carefully cared for, keeping them fed, watered and weed-free so they are never under stress. Plants are grown in traditional rows because it looks neat and tidy, sowing crops like lettuces and beetroot 'a little and often' so there is a regular supply and when the judges come in July there are vegetables at all stages of growth. You have to go round with them to explain what you've been doing and why. I garden organically, grow pest resistant varieties and keep a close eye on slugs. It's a great idea to cover the allotment with fleece when the seeds are sown, it stops all the pests from damaging them when they're young. You have to put the time in but I really enjoy it; lots of titivating is the key!

I'd won the local best plot on the allotment prize seven times, then one year one of the judges suggested that I enter the national competition. The night before it was judged a chicken escaped from a plot nearby, the owner found it early next morning scratching and digging away on the plot, he caught it, tidied up the plot but didn't dare tell me what had happened. It was two weeks before the results arrived and the fear of it affecting my chances made him ill, but he needn't have worried.

I was the first lady to win it and was speechless, it was so exciting, it just didn't sink in and the phone didn't stop ringing; I didn't go out for two days! There were pictures in the local paper, when the television phoned for an interview I thought it was just the kids having a laugh and I daren't tell you what I said, bottles of wine were left in my poly tunnel, someone gave me champagne and there were lots of cards. I didn't realise just what I'd done, it's still difficult to believe. I did my best and won the first time I entered, life can't get better than that!"

BRIAN OF BRITAIN

Just after the Second World War Brian Taylor, then aged 15, completed one of his first inventions, creating a television from a piece of army surplus equipment. Even now his mind still fizzes with creativity. "I have a hundred good ideas a day, and if one a week turns into something useful, I've actually done quite well!" he confesses.

A solar powered, self-winding hosepipe and cold frames with heat sensors have sprung from his fertile mind onto the reality of his allotment, but one of his greatest success is the automatic chicken coop gate with a light sensitive switch that opens the door in the morning and closes it at night. "It protects my precious poultry from foxes and saves me the job of trudging to and fro night and morning to open and close the hatch which is something of a chore in winter." Power for his projects comes from solar panels on the

shed roof. "They came from the days in the early 80's when I was involved with designing a solar powered telephone for a coastguard station on the Norfolk coast, these are the original panels, and still work perfectly, providing sufficient energy, even in winter. Recycled windscreen wiper motors provide the power for most of my inventions, I used to pick them up at car boot sales but have now found a source on the internet and they're really cheap."

The cold frame comprises three 4 x 5 foot bays covered with counterbalanced glazed frames. A windscreen wiper motor is connected to a

temperature sensitive module and a winding mechanism raises or lowers the panes according to the temperature. He has even modified the design of the traditional compost bin design by making interlocking concrete beams which can be built up as the heap rises. Others are lined with two inch sheets of polystyrene stuck to a wooden frame that improves heat retention and helps the compost to cook.

"Most of my developments are as a result of trial and error, I am a fairly optimistic sort of chap and don't get too downhearted. It's part of the development process. Most recognise the benefits of my inventions but I suspect one or two put me in the 'Heath Robinson' category, I don't mind, in my world it's almost a compliment!"

Beacon Hill
Allotment & Leisure
Gardeners Society

GARDENING IN A ROUNDABOUT WAY

Ernie Brown is on a mission, he started the incredible edible roundabout to advertise the Beacon Hill Allotment site in Cleethorpes, and won't give up until all the plots are filled. The roundabout is packed with colour, he's tried gorgeous crimson flowered broad beans, kale with purple leaves and bright yellow blooms, leeks and chives for their flowers and globe artichokes too. "Most of it's a blur as people in cars drive past, they don't want detail, just shapes and blocks of colour. Sometimes they stop their car on the roundabout for a chat or shout 'it's looking really good today' as they go by. I visit every day and bring my tools on my bike, which has an electric motor to make life easier. My hoe has lots of different heads, they all go with the watering can in the front basket and I hold onto the handle with my hand.

I love my allotment, it's my passion. We have an astronomy hut on the site, with a roof that spins round like the one in Felix the Cat. I've got a big shed too, with a stove, bed, table and chairs and rocking chair, I could quite happily live there, just for the summer. I've mentioned it to the missus but she's not keen!"

ALLOTMENT LIFE

Allotment holder and singer/songwriter Sally Goldsmith found enough allotment inspiration to record a CD and create a touring show called 'Plotters'. It is based around allotment experiences in Sheffield, where many of the sites are set on hillsides with views over the city, a wonderful combination of industrial architecture and enclaves of green to the rugged moorland beyond. "I met a vast cross-section of society, young and old, miners, solicitors, children, poets and artists; all excited by the thought of 'a little piece of country in the town'. Allotments are a celebration of imagination and human diversity, where you can be an 'urban peasant' and stamp your own personality on your plot in a neutral environment, away from the pressures and constraints of everyday life. There is the freedom to express yourself, indulge in creative fantasies and be in control; it's not about money so the imagination clicks in instead. Most people describe allotment life as a tonic to revive their physical and mental health. I met a husband and wife with four allotments who took on the first while both recovered from cancer, discovered a group of visually impaired people who cultivate the soil and their friendships while helping one another and an ex-tax inspector who grew cannabis as a herbal remedy for his wife who had M.S. There's a sense of anarchy too, an artist simply 'planted' rows of umbrellas and a group of teenagers who used their plot as a place to hang out, just dug an enormous hole! Then there was a lady who built a fantastic toilet on her allotment that became her 'throne' room. She and her partner have a 'respite corner' complete with lawn, garden gnomes and a place where they bury their pets.

Some allotments are smart, others, scruffy. A few allotments in Sheffield were full of pigeon lofts, but the 'fanciers' were always getting into trouble with the local authority, they weren't interested in the ground and spent their time looking at the sky, they could recognise their pigeons winging their way over the landscape from miles away. Pigeons are as much part of the allotment tradition as are growing brassicas or carrots, but they aren't the only livestock. Out on the 'wild west' of Sheffield there's a private allotment where people keep animals. One bloke kept a goat, pigs, dogs and a pony, he'd been a butcher all his life and was used to keeping animals on marginal land within the city and continued the practice in retirement. Another site had been derelict apart from a plot belonging to an old boy, Bert, the sole survivor of a once thriving site who was left alone in the middle, defiantly making a last stand against the encroaching weeds. One day, to his surprise, the community got together and resurrected the site, now it's pristine, supported by the 'locals' and a fantastic facility.

I also heard about a Guy Fawkes night party at an allotment, where they turned an old caravan into a burger bar. The bonfire was so huge that someone called the fire brigade who arrived, sirens blaring, checked the fire was OK and ended up staying for fireworks and burgers!

There was plenty of material for 'Plotters', much to my relief, the 'allotmenteers' who've seen it really enjoyed the show. When we went on the road, rural audiences were fascinated by the urban allotment experience. Allotments are extraordinary centres for self expression and seem to attract characters, no wonder they're such a great place for stories!"

GETTING STARTED ON THE ALLOTMENT

- Take it easy, dig over your plot little by little. Try and do everything at once and you may overdo it and lose your enthusiasm.

- Make sure your soil is well prepared before planting; add well rotted organic matter, leaf-mould and homemade compost to enrich the soil.

- 'Sow as you go' in newly prepared ground, tasting your first home-grown vegetables is a great incentive to carry on digging.

- If you're new to the allotment game, use a medieval method to find out if the soil is warm enough for seeds to germinate. Sit on it with your bare bottom, if it is too cold for comfort, seeds won't germinate!

- Train your partner to do domestic chores then you can spend more time on your plot.

- Grow potatoes in newly dug ground, the constant cultivation of 'earthing up' and dense foliage cover keeps weeds under control.

- See what's flourishing on nearby plots before selecting varieties to grow.

- Take advice from old sages; then do your own thing!

- Sharing an allotment with friends reduces the workload and doubles the fun!

- Don't take failures personally, learn from them and become an expert!

BLOOMIN' MARVELLOUS

"I grow my roses in Ramsbottom, it's the heart of rose growing country" announces Tony Bracegirdle who has been growing them there for forty years. "I now have 1,002 plants, from ramblers to miniatures, growing on my allotments because the garden is too small and the collection is still growing! Here on the western slopes of the Pennines, conditions are moist and reasonably cool, encouraging constant slow growth so blooms are more refined. They are 'budded' onto my own rootstock which performs best in our conditions. The soil is improved with well rotted horse manure, there's a watering system from a nearby spring that is 98% pure and slightly acidic, and I start spraying before pests and diseases appear. I believe that this and plenty of dedication gives me the edge in competitions.

I was nervous about entering the big shows but came away with a first and a second at the first attempt and was hooked! I have won the British National Amateur Championship eleven times since, my wife Alice helps and is very much part of the success. The competition is judged on the first, middle and last shows of the season and in 2006 I amassed enough points in the first two to win it, but I'm not going to retire! Anyone who wants to be champion will have to take it from me! I enter about twenty five shows each year from the end of June until the end of September. 'Admiral Rodney' is always the first to flower and fragrance and the last is 'Debby Thomas'; there are sixty of each rose on the plot so only the best blooms are chosen.

One of my favourites is good old 'Fragrant Cloud' for its scent, 'Wimi' and 'Pink Favourite' are disease resistant. 'Red Devil', an older variety that is still winning gave me one of my most memorable moments. The Great Lakeland Rose Show was being opened by Princess Grace of Monaco and the Red Devils Parachute team were there too. When they jump out of the aircraft they link hands then pass a rosewood baton around the circle, when it gets back to where it started they break the circle and open their parachutes. There was a 'Red Devil' class at the show and they said they would present their baton to the winner. I had one and Princess Grace of Monaco had another. I really treasure it!

The greatest disappointment was coming second when there was a greenhouse on offer and I really needed one. I asked the judge 'why?' and was told that the top two were inseparable so he turned the exhibits round and on the back of mine there was a spider. That spider cost me a greenhouse!"

FAYRE EXCHANGE

"The first ever 'Big Food Swap' was a great success" exclaimed Julie Waddicor enthusiastically ,"I'm really looking forward to the next one. The event is being held over consecutive weeks at three of our best allotment sites and a library, to try and reach a different audience. People brought garlic, shallots, lots of lettuces, dahlias, sweet peas, honey and some of the largest marrows I've ever seen! It was really exciting. People swapped, then waited around to see if something else came along then swapped again; some produce changed hands several times! It was a chance to catch up with the gossip too; there's lots going on! One site has a couple of naked gardeners who've planted a big hedge around their plot to maintain their privacy, another chap buried his pet horse on his plot using a JCB because he didn't know what to do with it, there's affairs going on in sheds, and while that's all going on they still have time to grow lots of fabulous vegetables for the Big Food Swap. All human life is there!"

ANIMAL MAGIC

"It started as a wind up" reveals Eric Horton, Field Secretary of the Castle Hill Allotments in Ipswich. "A lady on our allotment site wanted to keep animals, but she already had the maximum number of chickens and rabbits and it wasn't possible for her to keep any of the other animals she wanted, so I made the head and shoulders of a gorilla eating a banana out of papier mache and stuck it in the compost heap. Now I'm making an animal every two weeks and have a greenhouse full of them. There are snakes, a chameleon, giraffe and monkey. They have been weather-proofed with varnish and stay on the allotments all year round, and we also have some plastic and inflatable dinosaurs too! The children often give me designs, I make the animal then hide it in our wildlife area for them to find, they sometimes return the joke too! There are five scarecrows leftover from a competition, including a spaceman and a six foot four second world war soldier on sentry duty, complete with home guard helmet, who is known as 'Pete the Pill Box guardsman'. The site is alive with flags too, it's an impressive sight. The first to go up was the flag of St George, a gentleman whose house looked over the field came over and complained about it and within two weeks the site was covered with them!

We find lots of fossilised sea anemones and shark teeth from the ice age on the site and keep a pot full in a shed; when newcomers arrive we scatter them round their plot, tell them the story and it's dug within a week! We want to make this a community allotment where anyone can come, grow a few vegetables and a good time is had by all!"

BEST VEGETABLES TO GROW

- Runner beans – tops for taste and the sign of summer. Cultivar 'Red Rum' can be a problem, it keeps on jumping over the fence!

- Tomatoes – tantalising, tasty and easy to grow; every plot should have some!

- Peas – perfection in a pod; eat them raw, straight from the vine.

- Sweetcorn – take it straight from the plot to the pot for maximum flavour.

- Potatoes – out with the old and in with the new. Scrumptious!

- Carrots – eat them fresh to capture the crunch!

- Onions – know them and you've got it made.

- Lettuce – purple, chocolate, lime and speckled; great to bring colour to seasonal salads.

- Beetroot – bright and beautiful beet tastes delicious in a fresh bean salad.

- Courgettes – low calorie, colourful and easy to grow.

BEST FRUITS AND FLOWERS TO GROW

- Sweet peas – an allotment classic for flower and fragrance. The more you cut, the more you get.

- Gladioli – beloved of allotment gardeners; Dame Edna's favourite!

- Chrysanthemums – favoured for their timeless charm.

- Nasturtiums – edible flowers and leaves, and to keep 'black fly' from your broad beans.

- Dahlias – from bold and blowsy to pretty little pom-poms these brazen beauties have got the lot.

- Strawberries – quintessential summer fruits. How many would you like? Forty love!

- Raspberries – "a man who is tired of raspberries is tired of life". 'Autumn Bliss' more than lives up to its name!

- Pears – sink your teeth into a perfect pear and you'll be hooked – forever!

- Gooseberries – an old favourite – perfect for fools.

- Plums – 'Victoria', 'Czar' and the 'Grand Duke' flourish in 'Merryweather'.

PLOTTING FOR THE FUTURE

In the past few years the Sevenoaks allotment holders site has been revitalised under new leadership, changing from a site in decline to one that's opened under the famed National Gardens' Scheme. "Not long ago we were short of numbers and much of the site was overgrown, now we're forging ahead" says committee member Andy Garland enthusiastically. "Opening to the public is all part of the regeneration and we want to raise the profile, making it more of a community resource – the aim is to fill every plot. The whole 11.5 acres was opened as part of the 'Sevenoaks Festival'- the site has never looked so tidy! It was a chance for potential plot holders to see what was happening; visitors came from all over Kent and as far afield as Australia. As many plot holders as possible were on their site to chat or exchange advice with visitors, from novices to a couple with 97 years combined experience. Those who grew plants in raised beds or traditional straight lines, someone who has planted a vineyard and a couple of artists who have plots with a colour co-ordinated approach with pods, flowers and foliage in purple, mauve and crimson, linked with ornamental alliums.

The first time we opened we had 50 people and let some spaces but now with the help of the National Gardens' Scheme and their wonderful publicity machine we had 211 adults and masses of children. The aim is to continue improving the site and bring allotments into the 21st century where they belong, there is so much more we can do and it's very exciting."

LIFE ON THE TERRACES

Ian White is the vice-chairman of One Tree Hill Allotments on the side of a steeply sloped hill near Epping in London. He says "It's tough at the top for plot holders, there is no vehicle access, we thought of lifts or cable cars for shifting materials but in the end it's just sheer hard work, everything has to be carried up by hand. Most allotmenteers see it as a challenge to use their initiative. One employed a young relation to carry sacks of compost up the hill for an afternoon in return for some decorating and there are some fantastic examples of terracing! There is a transfer list for those who would like to move down the hill as they get older but most people stay at the top because of the views. It's not easy gardening on heavy clay on a slope. When people ask to be put on the waiting list, we send them an application form explaining the commitment that is needed to be successful – the couple who thought it would be great fun to bring a jazz band onto the allotment didn't last long! With care and cultivation the ground can be as productive at the top of the hill as the bottom – some people have spectacular results! One plot, packed with fruit trees and bushes, shows the most efficient way of making an allotment productive as it is less intensive than vegetable growing, and the gardener has won RHS medals for his fruit."

"I believe in composting, everything goes onto my heap, including hair and toenails! We have the usual problems with pests and diseases. When we suffer from potato blight, the plots at the top of the hill get it a day or two earlier so they alert the people at the bottom that it's coming. I run a beer festival in June and get quite a bit of sludge, so my beer traps are well stocked for the summer. My favourite fruit is the apple - when it's turned into cider! We spend a day on the allotment in autumn, pressing apples and drinking apple juice, what's left is taken home and made into cider for the spring; we're thinking of developing a community orchard." Now that's a great idea!

COLLECTIVE ENDEAVOURS

"I met a group of people in a squat in the autumn of 1994 while protesting against the Criminal Justice Act and we decided to start an allotment" explains Warren Carter. "Our first on the site was given to us rent free for twelve months because it had been derelict for nearly twenty years, but we worked hard to clear it. We now have eight, taking almost all of the site and are officially known as the Moulsecoomb Forest Garden and Wildlife Project. There are wildlife areas and parts are uncultivated so we can picnic, sunbathe and bake potatoes in the fire. It's a community garden and open to the public who come and help in return for some organic produce.

We've created a forest garden, mimicking the natural layers found in a forest. There are apples, cherries, plums, damsons, mulberries, hazels and walnuts, with fruit bushes in the middle layer and over fifty different perennial crops and fungi at ground level. Nowadays fewer than twenty species of plants supply ninety percent of all our foods which is frightening, part of our ethos is to look to new crops that might be useful in the future.

We have an outlawed vegetable plot too, growing seeds which are illegal to sell. Over 90% of all vegetable varieties have been lost in the last 100 years along with their genes for future breeding and we need to conserve what's left."

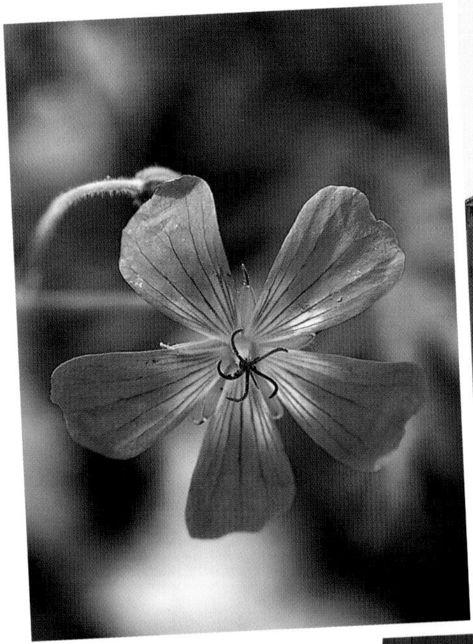

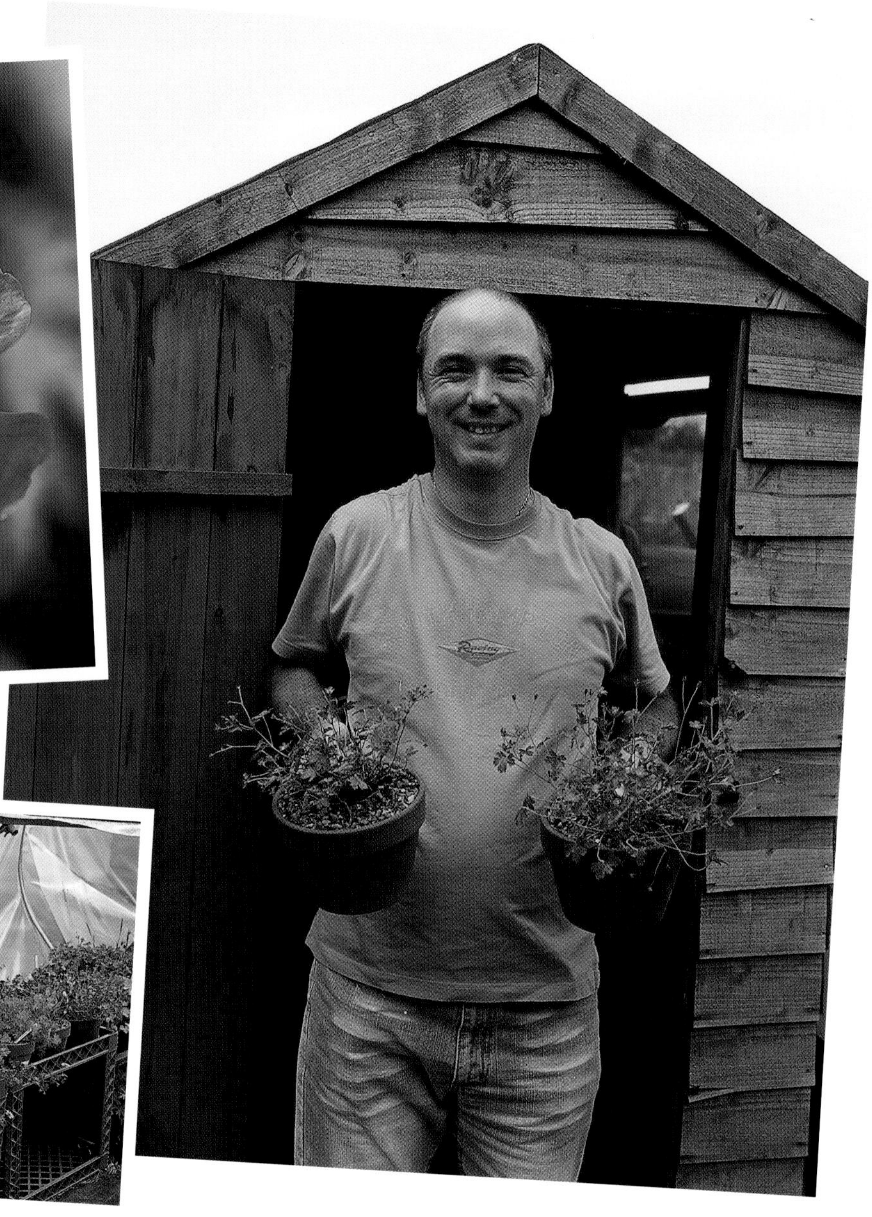

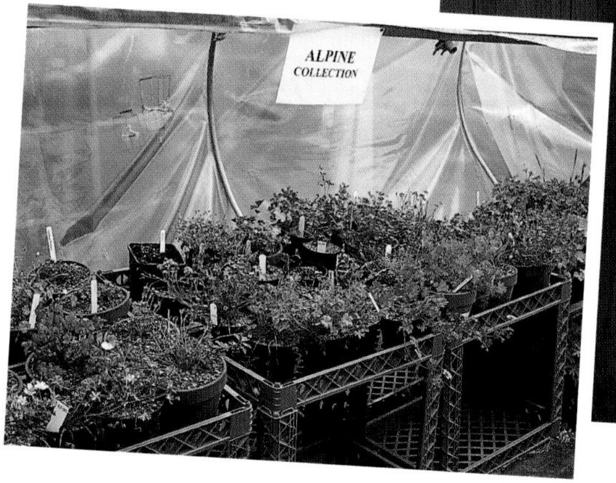
ALPINE
COLLECTION

HERBACEOUS HAVEN

"A house move forced me to pot up my entire collection of Hardy Geraniums, so I decided to take over an allotment and re-plant them there" explained Geranium Guru Gary Bartlett. "The allotment holders were bemused and tried to guess what I was doing. In spring as the foliage appeared, someone came and asked how many different types of strawberries I had, another asked 'Where's the potatoes?' they couldn't believe I would grow Geraniums on an allotment!

What started out as a hobby became a passion and there are now over 250 in the collection. They are planted in lines in alphabetical order with all of the different groups together, so it is easy to compare and contrast their characteristics. I have two polythene tunnels and a shade house for smaller alpine varieties that grow in terracotta pots. Geraniums are so easy to manage, the outdoor area is covered with weed suppressing fabric to keep the weeds down and control moisture, they are cut down in winter and mulched with forest bark and are rarely watered because the soil was enriched when vegetables were grown there in the past.

I love Geraniums because of their variety; white, pink, blue, purple flowers with a range of markings, from alpines to four foot high scramblers, leaf colours from green to variegated, blotched, brightly coloured in spring. I've met some fabulous people because of them. To be honest, they've changed my life, I'd be lost without my Geraniums!"

EVERY SECOND COUNTS

"My motto is 'if it is good enough to eat, it's good enough to show' " reveals passionate plot-holder Matt Baldwin. "I did well in my first competition, won several top prizes and three cups so I decided to carry on. I was doing quite well with my carrots one year until someone sabotaged the beds with growth retardant! I start plants off as much as possible in a cool greenhouse because the weather is so variable early in the year and the growing conditions are controlled for the best quality growth. I've selected my own varieties of leeks, onions, beans and peas over the years to ensure they are the best I could possibly grow and they taste good too! I entered a national competition and came second – I couldn't believe it! The judging panel come round in July when allotments are at their peak. You have to be a good all rounder, they were looking for a weed-free plot full of good quality vegetables and fruit with everything correctly labelled and with space to grow. I've entered again this year, will I come first? Only time will tell!"

COMPOSTING TIPS

- Do it - you can never have enough heaps!

- Have several heaps at different stages of decomposition for a constant supply of goodness.

- Keep a pig or chickens, they turn everything into compost without having a heap.

- Recycle – hair, toenail clippings, old woollen and cotton clothes, cardboard, envelopes, paper towels and the fluff from the tumble drier all rot down rapidly.

- Make sure the heap is well mixed with soft and 'woody' material.

- Water in dry weather to hasten decomposition but protect from soaking rain.

- A layer of rabbit droppings is a good activator.

- Don't put meat scraps on the heap, it encourages flies and vermin.

- Sweep leaves from the streets to create rich, soil improving leaf mould.

- Put pee on the heap; the first of the day is best!

COMPETITION TIPS

- Don't take it too seriously – just make sure you win!

- Save only the best for showing.

- Rub leeks with baby oil to make them shine.

- Keep a diary of sowing, growing and harvest so plants peak in time for the show.

- Grow potatoes in leaf mould for a silky sheen to the skin.

- Harvest runner beans over several days, wrap them in a tea towel and put them in the fridge to stay fresh.

- Discard carrots with green shoulders.

- Spray cauliflower curds with water just before judging.

- Ensure your exhibits are blemish-free.

- Whatever you do, don't get caught!

FLOWER POWER

Margaret was brought up on a farm in Ireland and started gardening as a child, so kitchen gardening is in her blood. "I have the best soil on the site, it looks like something that has come straight from a compost bag and it produces lots of lovely fruit and vegetables, so for a vegetarian like me, it's perfect.

I like to brighten up the plot; there are new colour schemes every year, it may be white and blue or green and yellow, whatever takes my fancy. Three of my plots are decorated with flower people, the shape is cut out with a jig saw and the clothes are painted on. The man, holding a pot of flowers, has a head made from a flower pot topped with blue grass. There's also a lady with 'Ivy' hair and a life size figure of a flowerpot man with a cork for his nose and a straw hat and white gloves. I made them at home and drove them here with the flower pot man sitting in the front seat and the wooden man and lady lying down in the back! I got some funny looks at the traffic lights!

My first attempt at growing pumpkins was just for fun then someone suggested that it should go in our allotment competition. When it came to judging day, I couldn't shift it! Eventually several of my friends carried it off in a blanket, marching in just before the 'weigh-in' was finishing. People couldn't believe how big it was! It was lifted onto the scales using a fork lift truck but went right off the dial so my son took it to work in the back of his car to be weighed – it was 132 lbs! For ages two men had won it on alternate years then I stepped in and beat them both! I'm still the only woman to win it and my pumpkin still holds our record for the heaviest pumpkin! I gave it to the allotment and people bought the seed – it would have taken ages to eat it!"

GOING THE WHOLE HOG

"I was the first person to keep livestock on the allotment but now I'm not alone. You'll find chickens, sheep and goats on the Hampshire allotment site and there are so many animals that people often bring their children for an afternoon out to look round". Martin Aspin is particularly fond of his pigs. "I've kept Gloucester Old Spots, Saddlebacks, Middle Whites and Large Blacks for about ten years, they're all great characters. A few old chaps on our allotment still get together twice a day for a cup of tea and are rallied by blowing a whistle. The first blast means 'I'm putting the kettle on', the second means 'tea's brewed'. One day, about six of them had just sat down in their little shed when right on cue after the second whistle an old sow who had just escaped, wandered in and sat down. It was just as though she thought, 'Oooh, I fancy a cup of tea' and went in to join them! Another time she escaped and went through the narrow doorway into a small

greenhouse, where there was no room for her to turn round and come out. As we stood round scratching our heads deciding what to do, she slowly and carefully reversed out without doing any damage and happily walked away wondering what all the fuss was about.

My children love our pigs, we buy them as piglets; they play and roll around with them from the start and lie on each others tummies, pigs seem to have a sixth sense about children and are very tolerant, I've never had any problem with them at all. They are so cheap to feed, all our scraps and excess vegetables are

fed to the pigs and we get the manure to put back onto the allotment, so it's ultra-efficient recycling. The phrase 'piggy bank' comes from keeping a pig, people would invest their money in a pig, fatten it up and have it killed. They would then cash in their investment from the meat. The pigs have a happy life and we end up with ham, sausages and salami and if there is any left over, we exchange our meat with other allotment holders.

The combination of pig and chicken manure is very potent, I was carefully nurturing an 'Atlantic Giant' pumpkin for a competition, but didn't know there was another hiding behind the compost heap which was taking all the run off that had become a high octane liquid feed. One day I popped round the back and was confronted by an absolute monster, the one I nurtured, less than half the size, was immediately abandoned in favour of my new found giant that eventually weighed a staggering 24 stone and took four of us to carry it off in a tarpaulin!"

PICKLED PUMPKINS

A chance meeting with the 'Blue Peter' gardener gave Terry a top tip for growing giant pumpkins. "The secret is to use beer. I started feeding them occasionally with old bottles that were knocking about the house. My first attempt grew to 35lbs and went to a local charity for a 'Guess the Weight' competition. The next year I sent off for some giant pumpkin seeds from Canada, a selection of 'Dill's Atlantic Giant'. I told the landlord of my local and he started giving me the leftovers of the barrels to feed it, finally he gave me the barrel too, which was put alongside the pumpkin plant with a pipe leading into the ground. It ended up 'supping' six pints of beer every other day and growing to 175lbs, people came from miles around to see this amazing beer drinking pumpkin! It went to raise money for a school for children with learning difficulties, they had a 'guess the weight competition' then hollowed it out into a Halloween lantern and

people threw money into it. The next year I went back to ask for some seed and they charged me £1!

The first year it was transported to the 'weigh in' by four firemen who lifted it onto a tarpaulin and marched off under the blaze of television cameras onto the tender, which was escorted by police cars to the local hospital to be weighed on the patients' scales. The next year soldiers from the four Welsh Regiments came in an armoured vehicle and took it away to be weighed.

Pumpkin plants can be huge, so I don't grow them on my allotment anymore and the children have a plot of their own. The answer lies in the soil, if that is in good health with plenty of humus and worms, the plants grow really well. I'm not sure if the beer is a gimmick or not but you need six pints a day to keep a pumpkin happy!"

UNUSUAL VEGETABLES TO GROW

- Kohl-rabi – the legendary edible 'Sputnik'.

- Sweet Potato – a taste of the tropics for 'new wave' allotmenteers.

- Oca – tiny tubers from the Andes, eat when your potatoes peak.

- Cardoons – beloved by Victorians, but rarely seen today.

- Chayote – looks like a pear but is actually a cucumber!

- Jerusalem artichokes – good as a temporary windbreak!

- Salsify – known as the 'Vegetable Oyster' but not an aphrodisiac!

- Bitter Gourd – a strange looking fruit with skin like a crocodile, dice into curry or stuff with meat.

- Asparagus pea – ornamental and edible, what could be better?

- Soya beans – cold, hardy varieties mean better beans.

THE SWEET SMELL OF SUCCESS

"The Carshalton Lavender Project has re-planted lavender on three acres of derelict plots at Stanley Park Allotments", explains Roger Webb. "Around the 18th century, this area of Surrey was the lavender capital of the world. In 1749 Potter and Moore, famous distillers of lavender water, were based in Mitcham and it helped companies like Yardley establish their international reputation too.

We cleared the land of brambles and rubbish and engaged the expertise of a French horticulturist, Hervé le Reveron. The fields were established from around 22,000 cuttings taken from plants that still existed in local gardens which we found through adverts in the local press. The nearer we got to areas like Merton, the more prolific they became, this was the centre of the lavender industry. The cuttings were grown on by volunteers at nearby Downview Prison who also helped to clear the land.

Each year we harvest almost a ton of lavender. It takes a day to cut and is a long way from the time when men, women and children would work fourteen hour days using small steel sickles. It produces up to ten litres of distilled oils which is then sold through local outlets and farmers' markets. The fields have become a local attraction. Once a year we have an open weekend, it's 'pick your own', all you have to do is bring your scissors! The project has come to mean a lot to me; in this area everyone has some awareness of lavender – it is almost in your blood."

PUMPKIN PILE UP

Tereshina Roberts, a Brazilian artist and passionate gardener, loves pumpkins, gourds and squashes. She cooks with them and has them all round the house as ornaments. "They remind me of home where they sell them on the side of the road. My favourite for ornaments is 'Turks Turban' it is such a wonderful shape and lasts so well". She has also used squashes in her art. At 'The Custard Factory' art centre in Birmingham, Tereshina created an aerial view of Spaghetti junction; serpentine 'Tromba d'Albegna' were jack-knifed lorries, two marrows end-to-end were articulated lorries, giant pumpkins became wide loads and smaller ornamental varieties, cars (see www.pumpkins.ik.com). Tereshina and thirty of her friends grew over 500 squashes for the display. "My friend Betty grew over 200 of them that were all taken to the art gallery by men from the council. They are so simple to grow, we took over two overgrown allotments to grow some of the plants, dug a hole for each one, watered them well and within days a mass of leaves and stems smothered the grass and weeds.

Visitors loved the art, they sat on the pumpkins, laid down next to them, thumbed lifts and laughed. It was interactive art from the allotment!"

HELP IS AT HAND

"'Growthpoint' is helping adults, who have mental health needs, to get involved in society and develop new skills in a supportive working environment." explains project manager, Geoff Yardley. "The site covers eleven allotments, has a vegetable plot and planting area with glasshouses, a polythene tunnel, composting area and a training room. There is plenty to do, from seed sowing to taking cuttings. We produce bedding plants, vegetables and a range of shrubs and perennials that are sold to the council to decorate their sites.

Horticulture is a leisurely occupation so you are never under stress. There is great reward for minimal effort – sow a tray of seeds and within weeks you have hundreds of plants in pots, so there's a high level of job satisfaction. I'm passionate about horticulture and this job, with all it's positives is the icing on the cake!"

Everyone who comes here loves the fresh air and open spaces. We're never short of volunteers when it comes to tasks like weeding and waterings, particularly when we are getting ready for open day. One of its highlights is the barbecue, sweetcorn tastes so delicious when it is picked and then cooked straight away. It's enough to make the Jolly Green Giant turn red with envy!

A LIFE LESS ORDINARY

Rob Foster was born to garden. His interest developed at school and by the time he was fourteen he was spending more of his days outside than in the classroom. He took charge of the school gardens and greenhouse, the potting shed and sports pitches. "People looked down on me for doing it", he recalls "but now everyone wants to garden, how times change! It's an interest that lasts a lifetime and you never cease to learn, particularly on the allotment". He now has six allotments that are ploughed with a classic Ferguson tractor, bought from a farmer. "My tractor is almost as old as me and was manufactured at Banner Lane, Coventry on Thursday 2nd September 1954, one of 269 made on that day and unlike myself, it still starts first time! I plough the plots for some older gardeners as well as my own, which supplies a wide range of vegetables for the pot and harvest festival produce for several inner city schools. Often the children can't believe what they're seeing, many of them think that vegetables come from a supermarket, they've never seen them engrained with soil before and are almost afraid to touch them.

A lifetime in horticulture has been fascinating and fulfilling, I met Prince Charles, manage several allotment sites, broadcast on the radio and am a National Vegetable Society judge. Competitors will try anything, I once found a carrot with a huge crack in it that had been filled with 'Mansion' furniture polish – the smell gave the game away – and people regularly glue the flowers onto cucumbers. Gardening is full of myths and trickery but you should try things out for yourself. It's a myth that planting carrots in freshly manured ground makes them 'fork', that water on the leaves causes scorching in sunshine and that potatoes should be planted on Good Friday – it was the only day off work in spring that our forefathers had". Bob has seen a lot too – "I once discovered a man growing 'Japanese Knotweed' to

provide shade on his allotment. He thought we were joking when we told him it is illegal." Travelling round allotments, Rob has noticed a change in clientele, "there are more young people and families these days which is good news for the future, yet the more things change, the more they stay the same. In 1944, Roy Hay's book recommended sand pits for the children, swings for those who were a little older and putting greens for the adults, to make them family friendly. Allotments are now appearing in new housing developments with facilities for children but we may have to wait a while for the putting greens!"

GIRLS JUST WANNA HAVE FUN!

Meet the 'Dirty Hoes' allotment club whose pseudonyms are Audrey, Margot, Dolly, Bubbles, Little Tarquers, Bunty (and a man called Monty who does the digging); who have a dedicated desire for 'fun and fresh produce!' Inspired by a collective dream of harvesting fresh vegetables, partaking of Pimm's on the patio and having a laugh, they spent their first winter evenings prior to planting enjoying red wine and crisps, studying books on vegetable gardening, deciding on the colour of the shed (lilac anyone?) and consulting the dictionary for definitions of gardening terms like 'mulching'.

"There are potatoes, rhubarb, onions, garlic, broad beans, French beans, runner beans, lots of tomatoes and fabulous fruit in the first year. We are already planning for year two and will be building raised beds from recycled timber to take the strain out of weeding. We've discovered new talents, Dolly is a wonder weeder (though her nails are atrocious), Margot is a seed sowing sensation and Bunty talks to tomatoes and makes them grow.

'Little and often', is our new mantra, for feeding, watering and harvesting, it's the only way to stay on top of the plots. ('No falling out, it's only an allotment!') We don't want 'perfect' vegetables – just to have fun while growing tasty, fresh, chemical free produce; and the satisfaction of side stepping the supermarkets!"

SNAKE CHARMER

Betty Farruggia is a big fan of 'Sicilian Snakes'. "I first heard about them from my Sicilian husband and thought they weren't available in Britain until one grew from a packet of mixed squash seeds. Since then, I've been hooked! They are such fun and easy to grow. I sow them in small pots in the greenhouse in early May and plant them out about 18 inches apart about three weeks later when the weather is warm. The ground is prepared several months earlier, digging a trench and enriching the soil with rotted manure, as you traditionally do for runner beans. People are surprised that they grow up canes rather than on the ground like courgettes. The snakes start off like thin courgettes, they can be eaten at this stage though I've never tried them, I prefer the larger fruits that are cooked like marrows or squashes. Fruits developing about 4 feet above the ground are the best, they curl upwards once they touch the soil and make fascinating shapes; the longest I have ever grown was over five feet long. People on my allotment site are fascinated by them, we're holding our first 'Longest Sicilian Snake competition', which is very exciting!

I love unusual vegetables, a friend of mine in San Diego told me about a strange squash from Mexico with fruit that look like pears and I recognised it as something that I'd seen for sale in a market in Birmingham, the West Indians use them in soups and call them 'Chocho'. I bought one and left it on a windowsill, first a root appeared from one end, then shoots at the other, so I potted it out and it grew rapidly and was grown in the same way as the 'Snakes'. They didn't produce fruits because I planted them too late but it is not a problem, I'll try them another year."

GETTING RID OF PESTS AND DISEASES

- Steep rhubarb in water in an old dustbin for six weeks and use the infusion to spray onto cabbages to discourage cabbage root fly and caterpillars.

- Squash small infestations of aphids as soon as they form or blast them off with a hose.

- Cover brassicas with a fire guard to protect them from pigeons.

- When setting beer traps for slugs, stout or alcohol-free is the weapon of choice.

- Counteract club root by adding lime to the plot and planting hole.

- If you're new to the plot, find out prevalent pests and diseases – prevention is better than cure.

- Put bird-boxes on your plot, blue tits love aphids and codling moth caterpillars.

- Spray mildew with milk, up to a 30% dilution in water will magic it away.

- Whenever possible, buy disease-resistant varieties.

- Knock the leaves of affected plants and suck up the whitefly in a portable vacuum cleaner.

JOBS THROUGHOUT THE YEAR

January – Shred and rot down your Christmas tree and use it as mulch.

February – Apply general fertiliser to fruit bushes and trees.

March - Plant shallots.

April - Hoe, Hoe, Hoe.

May – Don't harvest asparagus from plants that are less than two years old.

June – Pinch out side shoots on tomatoes.

July – Pick courgettes before they become marrows.

August – Plant especially prepared potatoes for Christmas.

September – Cut out the canes of summer fruiting raspberries.

October – Divide rhubarb crowns to make more plants.

November – Dig, dig, dig, dig, dig, dig, dig, the whole day through.

December – Harvest Brussels sprouts and pull parsnips for Christmas dinner.

IT'S A FAMILY AFFAIR

It's not unusual to find ten children working together on a produce packed allotment in the picturesque village of Flamstead. "When everyone's here, there's hardly enough room for us all", laughs Caroline Freer, one of four Mums in this happy family affair. "We took on an allotment so we could grow organic vegetables and brought the children along too for some fresh air and exercise. It is a great way to teach them about the origins of food and the importance of caring for the environment, you'd never think of an allotment being an educational aid. They love sowing seeds, monitoring what comes up, then weeding, watering and watching them grow. It's really caught their imagination, the older children have started putting in requests for plants, one is growing his own rhubarb, another wanted seeds for a pumpkin, and butternut squash and raspberry canes have been popular too.

They love eating vegetables straight from the plant, especially peas, tomatoes and green beans and often ride their bikes round the site scrounging produce from other allotment holders to top up their tummies. They seem happier to eat them when they're cooked too, it makes meals more exciting when you've grown your own and the guinea pigs love our leftovers. Growing vegetables has been an education for us all. When dung was delivered to the allotment during our first year, we thought it was rhinoceros poo from the local wildlife park and my husband now knows that 'Brussels' come on a stalk, not in a net bag from the supermarket!"

DEDICATION & ACKOWLEDGEMENTS

To my mother Marion, who loves her garden.

My thanks to Carolyn Hutchinson for thinking of me, all of the contributors for giving of their time and allowing us to use their stories, to Ruth Hamilton for her editorial skills and Paul Wright for perfection in design, to John Baxter and Suzie Gibbons for inspiring images, to Hazel Kirkman for her powers of production and Rosemary Wilkinson for Editorial Direction. To Gill for her help with transcribing the interviews and proofreading the text, and finally to Noel Greenwood for teaching me the importance of going the extra mile with a smile!

The publishers would like to thank the following people for supplying photos for use in the book: Ernie and Jacquie Brown (Gardening in a Roundabout Way), Terry Walton (Pickled Pumpkins), Mike Roberts and Eddie Campbell (Pumpkin Pile Up), Betty Farruggia (Snake Charmer).

Photographic credits:
John Baxter: p2, 4, 11, 22–24, 26–31, 46–47, 64–65, 66–69, 80
Suzie Gibbons: p7, 12–19, 32, 36, 38–41, 42, 44, 50, 52–55, 60, 70, 76
Ernie and Jacquie Brown: p20
Eddie Campbell: p62
Betty Farruggia: p8, 72
Mike Roberts: p62
Terry Walton: p57–58

Published in 2007 by
New Holland Publishers (UK) Ltd
London • Cape Town • Sydney • Auckland
www.newhollandpublishers.com

Garfield House
86-88 Edgware Road
London W2 2EA
United Kingdom

80 McKenzie Street
Cape Town 8001
South Africa

14 Aquatic Drive
Frenchs Forest, NSW 2086
Australia

218 Lake Road
Northcote, Auckland
New Zealand

ISBN 978 1 84537 684 0

Editor: Ruth Hamilton
Designer: Paul Wright
Photographers: John Baxter and Suzie Gibbons,
 except where stated on page 78
Production: Hazel Kirkman
Editorial direction: Rosemary Wilkinson

10 9 8 7 6 5 4 3 2 1

Reproduction by Modern Age Repro, Hong Kong
Printed and bound by Craft Print International,
 Singapore